The Artist

The Artist

Ruby Solly

TE HERENGA WAKA
UNIVERSITY PRESS

Te Herenga Waka University Press
Victoria University of Wellington
PO Box 600 Wellington
teherengawakapress.co.nz

A catalogue record is available at the National Library of New Zealand

ISBN 9781776920709

Published with the support of a grant from

Printed in Singapore by Markono Print Media Pte Ltd

For Waitaha, Kāti Māmoe and Kāi Tahu
and for all those whose ways of being have been misunderstood

Whakamārama

This kōrero contains mātauraka from manuscripts, conversations and mentoring by our tāua and pāua, and the many carriers of our knowledge and mahi toi within our rohe. It contains atua and characters from our shared whakapapa as Waitaha, Kāti Māmoe and Kāi Tahu, as well as specific tributes to tīpuna such as Hinepūnui—a name that has passed down through my whānau and wider whānau, and a name that I am proud to carry. But even though this story has been woven from truth—from kōrero and mātauraka treasured for generations—it is a kōrero pakiwaitara, a work of fiction derived from treasured mātauraka.

This book is a mahi aroha to the iwi that have shaped my being, and is an invitation to readers who whakapapa to the great Te Wai Pounamu to open the door into the wider world of our iwi and our knowledge. I pray that each taoka mātauraka, each reference and kōrero, inspires you to journey further for more knowledge of who we were and who we are as a people so that you become a greater resource for our mokopuna than any book could ever be. There are many worlds and realities that exist within our dreams of the taoka our ancestors left behind for us; this is just one of them.

For those who do not find comfort within this tale, I hope that there are other places that make you feel held within your mātauraka and tīpuna, and that one day we will all get to feel the safety and comfort that comes with being held within all the different stories we as a people are blessed to hold.

Contents

Kōrero Tuatahi

In which the world is sung into being, a land called Waitaha is carved by its people, iwi named Kāti Māmoe and Kāi Tahu arrive amidst fighting, a massacre takes place, Pākehā arrive, land is stolen, reparations are sought, and the people find peace within new pā where the land bears the scars of the recent past and ongoing present.

Kā Kaitapere

Players

The Artist

Hana

Hinepūnui

Sing

At the start there is nothing but black sand
except it is wider than we can know,
deeper than we can feel.
In fact, we are not yet a *we*,
       but are within it,
       the pulse of potential.

Maybe instead it is a black river
filled with tiny beings that move in circles
over and over, koru-spiralling vertebrates.
       But even they do not exist yet.

No, it is not a river
but a burning,
a fiery chain extending back and forth
deprived of colour,
fuel eternal underneath miles
and miles of pitch and peat.
       Except nothing has been alive to rot
       and live again as flame.

It is not a fire, either.
Perhaps it is the water that lives
inside the body—
the memories of the amniotic,
undrying pools of tears for things forgotten.

Then something begins to grow
but it doesn't come to form in the eye.
It's the almost-seen,
the shimmering of light that comes
after looking too closely at the sun.
The light particles that shiver upwards
when you gaze at sacred ground.

They are alive
in the potential of what comes first.
A gentle song emerges
so bright that sound becomes sight.
Thousands of sound icicles
trickle down the new world
as it is being made.
The creaking of ancient trees
that predate their maker;
they are only the thought of trees,
the potential of growth.
   And so from the black
      the world is sung
         into being
           not for us
             but for itself
              but for
               the song.

He Ao He Kōpae

The world is a disc
made of stone,
> sand,

> water,

> and women
living on the sand bank
placed grain by grain
> by the song.

It whispers into their heads,
> *Sing us into the wind,*

> *sing the winds into being*
and so the primordial mother
of the wind goddesses
weaves tāwhiriwhiri
for her daughters
placed in all directions
of the primeval compass.
> *Sing us into the wind,*
says the song,
with the gentle backing
of tumutumu *tap-tap-tap*
in each consonant.

Hinepūnui-o-Toka,
te pū o te hau,
gifts each daughter a fan
woven from the song,
its raki sung through every fibre,
through the very cells she was made from.

And so each daughter sings her verse:
> Hine-Roriki,

> the northern winds powerful and wild.

Hine-Rotia,
    the daughter held in the west.
Hine-Hauone,
    pressing the sands into their bank.
Hine-Aroraki,
    the one who holds the birds in place.
Hine-Aroaro-Pari,
    the one sister who rests on land
    singing the echoes of the world
    again   and again   and again.

    She hears herself becoming quieter
    with each repetition
until something changes deep within her waters. The current turns
           . . . in the reverse
in the last whispers of the echo
the song returns;
    There is a time where this is happening again,
she says
as it rises from the land
in shimmers of light
    tūtūmaiao,
        whiti te rā
as it is sung in as many ways
as there are voices
knowing that it will be sung
again   and again   and again
    until
the new fates emerge
        here
          in Waitaha.

Rākaihautū

Before we were men
we were bigger than men.
Bigger even
than the mana of women.
            Tipua foot falls
                on these fresh lands
kurī running
for the hills.
Ghosts of men
whispering through kōauau
just strings of air
through flute-like cocoons,
                melody incubators
                for fairy folk
moth flutters overtaking their raki,
with footprints never found.
All while Rākaihautū te tipua
            carved out our landscape
                with his kō,
                        Tuhiraki.
        The channels
                filled slowly
                    with the tears of Aoraki
                        and his brothers
                    frozen to stone mountains
                        on the back
                        of their father's new wife.

            Kā tipua,
    the link between the supernatural
            and us humans
            filtering down

            till there we were.

Our iho makawe flashing
as we chased tohu

into the bush.

Waitaha

Ko Uruao te waka,
and so we came.

    Like Rākaihautū
    we carve the land with our kō.

    Plantations in long lines
    etched into our skin.
    The hopes of Roko
    with gentle lines to follow
    the *tap-tap-tap*
    of toroa chisel.
    Long lined
    meditations in the mind
    to guide the hands.

        It is the song
        in its notation.
        On the surface
        just charcoal and shark oil swirling.
            But look closer,
            see the minuscule variations,
            the human touch of imperfection
            creating music.
            The notes between the notes;
                the mountains and the plains,
                the contrast in vibrato.
                We are becoming
                    ourselves.

            As taniwha of green richer
            than any forest
            swirl in rivers
            so cold

they turn men to stone.
By them
we are both frightened
and protected.

The kūmara grows
in times of peace.

Kāti Māmoe

Let us say this—
the north too is a world of its own.
On clear days
we would look to them
        and feel them
         look back at us
as we stood on our mountains
but never too close to the top.
    He ūpoko
    He tapu
    The sacred head of the brother shall stand

                  untouched.

We feel the line
    invisible
      but ever present.
        Tangible
          and complex.
            At first the aho is slack,
               a weight dragging
                  under the skin of the ocean,
              a discomfort,
          a warning.
      Then it is a taut line,
    pulsating
  as they pull themselves
to our shores.
    Hoea, hoea, hoea rā.

        We were an Us and a Them.
        Four generations
            gave themselves
        until this whawhai
          was woven

into the faces of the children
who held a hand from each of us
as they moved towards te ao mārama
Roko gazing upon us
his hands guiding us
to the caves.
Plain slates daunting us
with the ache of potential.

Then one emerges.
We will call him
The Artist.

He watches our fires
suffocate to embers.
Collects the ashes
as we sleep in despair.
Mixes them with shark oil,
bird fat,
and paints
what we dream.

Inside our histories,
we awaken.
Rākaihautū
strong above our heads.
Bird-like men
flying our hopes
back to Hawaiki.

The Artist sleeps from exhaustion,
a feather
pulling gently

through his shoulder blade.

Metamorphosis

piercing through

the skin.

We listen
to echoes of unseen folk
from the hills.
Gruff voices
of rocks clicking
in the hand.
The soprano of
kōauau
rising around small forest fires
dotting the furthest hills.
     So we still live
     the life of Roko.
     Slowly the red dust settles.
     Kōkōwai from our shared mother
     drifts down over our lands.

We take our enemies-turned-brothers
to see the Artist.
Show them the tīpuna
our children will share.
Trace the space inside his work,

                    te takata

               where the wairua lives.
            Feel it flow
         from the brush
      to the stone.

They take
the deep red earth

of every woman.
Mix it again
with the oil of our animals
and paint the awa atua,
        paint the separation of celestial beings,
          the taniwha that guards us all.

Kāi Tahu

We feel it
growing in the air around us.
Harmonics above pulling us to the hills
                        Here they come,
                            Here they come.

Tākitimu waka,
capsized mountains
both here and not here
in this place where time kisses itself
like old lovers finding each other
for the first time.

The arrival of Kāi Tahu
a dance between
                    Them and Us.
We move around one another,
                    barely touching
                        then all at once;
                                    electric
                        then electrified.

                    The woman they call mad,
                    all tousled hair and wide eyes,
                    crosses the mountains
                    with that hard stone, pounamu,
                    held tight at her breast.
                    This stone with green water trapped within
                    the hair cut from Hinepounamu,
                    here to escape the sandstone woman, Hinehoaka
                    and her death of one thousand cuts.

The mad little woman
watches the men struggle through the wood.
She laughs   *Ha! Wood eaters . . .*

27

then reveals the pounamu to them
and the song rings out again.

Hinepounamu now has a new fear
He tākata, he tākata, he tākata.

But they make her travel wide,
make her beautiful *to them*, useful *to them*.
Split her into more parts than she has ever come from
whakapapa   expanding,
         light   in   a   void.

We come to call this place
                    Te Wai Pounamu.

Travelling over,
about, and through it

we find the safest lands
and build ourselves a nest
Kai-a-poi, Kai-a-poi,
with a river flowing around it,
     holding us in a cradle of water
       as the children sneak from the houses
       to play in the raupō
as the ahi kā burn
and so again
the Us becomes a We.

Whawhai

At first these are plentiful times;
food swings across the river
    Kai-a-poi, Kai-a-poi,
until the song brings itself forward again
in the sound of raupō in the wind.
    Hide the children, hide the children.
Some hear the song and listen,
but sadly other lines will be cut.
Families to become blunt hei toki,
no longer shaping the world.

    Then the men come.

    There is talk of stolen stone,
    of moko slipping from the face.
    Tools of the white man's war
    ring out,
    like stones
    dropping
    from the skies.

        One woman
        hides under the water
        breathing through a reed,
        then springs to kill the impostors
        again   and again   and again.

Over time
we have learnt to hold both Roko and Tū
both peace and anger
in our blood.
We possess a pile of kūmara
as well as a pile of bodies.

But we cannot tell which are ours
and which are theirs.

They kidnap our best
and we weep loud enough for them to hear
from their island prison.
The ground sours,
the song now
all descending lines and screaming;   a wail,
                                             a karaka to the dead.

Kāika

Again, we move.
For we are travellers,
seasonal occupiers,
guides, makers and healers
looking for the best kai,
the best stone,
      the best, the best, the best.
But we are hurting,
splintering   like   the   wood
that   will   never be   cut
with   those   hei   toki,
               blunted.

    The young bodies living behind our eyes
    we see as if in a black lake,
       drifting to each other but not reaching out.
    We wake often in cold sweats.

We begin to settle in our places:
       the ones who see kēhua find each other,
       the ones who cling to Roko find a place of their own,
       the ones who strive for more,
       and the ones who are taken by pale men
find places to grow themselves.
       To put down roots,
       to look at a patch of sky
       and be owned by it
       as much as we claim each patch of sky
       for ourselves.

    The song
            breaks itself   into parts.
    Harmonies   become new tunes
       of their own.

Pākehā

We do not remember the first of them
but we recall the sound:
language like ours but with words that fall like
      birds   shot
      from   the   sky.
Consonants tapping away at us,
             Tap-tap-tap.

      Beneath the skin,
      the new ones grow within us.
            Some men forget themselves,
            sell women for barrels.
      We sing to the ones inside,
      for they too
      are Waitaha, Kāti Māmoe and Kāi Tahu.
      Into pūmotomoto
      we whisper the song.
            The new father's sea shanties
            cutting our rhythms
            in   half
                        Whiria te mokopuna,
                        Whiria te tākata.

Confiscation

This for that,
     those for these . . .
We trade in things
we never knew we needed.
Blanket wrapped
we sit proud on the ātea,
all pounamu and pearls.

Here for there,
     here for these . . .
We do not own the lands
for we were sung from them.
Here we are all together
but these men
keep their minds closed
to the waves of song
crashing in.

Here for that,
     Here for this . . .
The spaces we stand in are shrinking.
Long mats of land curl up at the edges
rolling further and further in,
even our caves
now just shelter for cattle.

Here, there, everywhere.
     There, everywhere, here . . .
If we do not sell these lands,
they will take them
from the men who killed us.
We will feel the quickening
the constant drowning
of those trapped

in the black lake
of the mind's eye.

This for nothing,
          that for nothing,
there for nothing,
          here for nothing . . .
The song sings inside itself.
We feel it move
in the black trickling up
from the beginning
pooling in our minds,

          a blood-stained blanket.

Settling

We are donning our long skirts
for our children to hide behind.
The *swish swish* of fabric on thighs
the familiar sound of the tāwhiriwhiri
pushing the breeze through the wetlands.

Bodies
       still
           washed clean
                 in our rivers
              that over time
       become stained.
   Invisible colours
too dark and dirty
       for our dead
            to rest within.

       Families at the bottom of the pā
       migrate again
       to become foreign birds.
Those who stay lose their feathers
one by one
       some fallen,
           some plucked.

The skirts move through dirt roads.
The *swish swish*
of dust rising,
on the wind again   and again.

***

       Named for that ancient mother of the South,
       a wise tāua,

Hinepūnui,
lets her moko
Hana
cling to the dark fabric,
    her small hands pulling the cloth aside
        to find light behind the darkness.

        They are waiting
        for their inheritance.
        They are waiting
        to hear
        the song.

Kōrero Tuarua

In which a Southern woman and man are made, twins are born under suspicious circumstances, the new family is shunned by their community, and names are bestowed upon the children by their elderly grandmother.

Kā Kaitapere

Players

Hine

Hana found herself in caves.
This little girl with dust
eating at her knees.
At first she went for the feeling of shelter
that was owned by no one
but itself.

As she grew into her bones
she went there for the silence
punctured only
by the north wind
running through on ancient feet.
And as she became more of herself
she went not for the silence
       but for what she could fill it with.

      Notes soared
      at first from under her tongue,
      light and whispered,
      like kōauau on the wind.

      Then as her body began to fill its cocoon,
      the voice burrowed into her chest,
      to the walls of the heart
      beating again with that tumutumu
      tap-tap, tap-tap, tap-tap.

      In the streets she is the plume of the iwi.
      A black feather tinged with white
      tucked into the hair of her whānau,
             brushed and oiled.

      But in the cave,
      she is a woman formed from earth.

Her hands reach to shape herself
                    Tēnei au, tēnei au.
She sculpts her mouth
with the round contour of the hills
opens it like a cathedral door,
and with the red of the paintings
trapped in her lips and cheeks,

                              she *sings*

Tama

Matiu is a Southern boy,
the shadow of a Southern man.
He knows the stories eddying in his waters,
knows that the blood spilled on this land
is as much his own as the rivers he fishes.

He knows that the rivers inside his body
are nothing more than tributes
to the rivers that feed the landscape.

His father leads him in silence
through all that is theirs.
He holds each creature
in the parchment of his hands,
gives them to the boy to touch.

The man takes a moth
                gasps
watches it fly from his palm to the boy's cheek;
        Takata wairua . . .
and the boy feels the vibration of the wings
the green air around them
shimmering.
        Then he hears it,
                the song.

                At first
                he thinks it comes from the spirit lying in his palm
                but then he listens closer

                It is coming from the caves.
                It is coming
                        from inside his bones.

Whaiāipo

He is captured.
Not by foreign enemy
or the white men,
but by a song
spiralling out
from the source.
He wakes with the koukou
of the ruru.
Feels the rope of the song
around him
in all the parts
that can't be seen.
He moves through bush
with moonlight to guide him.
    A slow walk at first
    then the rope tightens
        and he is running
        towards *the raki,*
        towards *the song.*

Then he sees her
and asks himself,
    Is she ghost?
    Is she tipua?
And Hana walks to him
closer
    and closer
still singing
    growing quieter
        and quieter
        until she is whispering her song
            into his ear.

As it travels through him
he moves
past to future
and back again.

When she finally touches him
Hana is a Southern woman
            and Matiu is a Southern man.

Spark

Each night
their bodies crash like waves
    Te Pō Uriuri,
    the penetrating night,
    with the *tap-tap-tap*
    beneath woollen blankets.
    Skin to skin moving
    tectonic plates
    with Rūaumoko shaking
    underneath.
    Hinepūnui-o-Toka
    and all her daughters
    turn these two bodies
    into the centre of the compass.
    The storm's eye forms clear and bright.
    Subtle and glowing
    deep inside
        the song
            sings itself.

And when they roll into dreams
he sees her in a vision,
naked on the floor of their cave.
Te whē, the stick insect
crawls across her sleeping form.
The paintings above
float down like leaves
falling to rest
on her abdomen
as it rises and falls.

But behind Hana's eyes
all is still.

Silent.

    She sees nothing

    but deep

    dark green

        flowing

            on and on

            through time

Wairua

Hana traces fingers
across her abdomen.

Beneath the skin
the puna
of Hine-Te-Iwaiwa
springs forth,
circulates
in its own tide.
Oceanic wānaka
in a microcosm.

Te whare tākata,
    upstanding.
The eyes and soul form
cell by cell,   note by note.
       The waters
from both mother and father
dance to the *ta-tap*
ta-tap of the heartbeat.

         Wai-rua: two waters
         becoming one.
           Tihei mauri ora.
           And so,
           it is sung.
           And so,
           it is life.

Māhaka

Long ago
there was a fight between our gods.
All the god brothers screamed
and cried.
Hurled their children
at each other.
Used their creations
as weapons
for which they were never intended.

This could have gone on forever.

Hine-Pū-Te-Hue
took in all their mamae
and all their anger
to grow a new world
within herself.
A sphere rounding out
from deep in the pito,
and from that pain
she released a song
to calm the gods.

Hana swells
with this new world
but more so
than the other mothers
who walk with her
to wash their clothes
in the stream.
Hana's wise tāua,
Hinepūnui,
named for the wind mother
of the beginning,

presses her hands
into the orb
of flesh.
Gasps to herself as if a first breath.
Look,
she says, pointing at the outline
of bodies back-to-back

Māhaka—

there are two.

Tohu

The summer maiden in the sky
has turned from her lover.
      The winter maiden
      has embraced the sun
      once more.
      In Hana's waters
      the world turns.
            Currents move
                  around two hearts
                        emerging.
            Their wairua
            formed with their eyes
                  back when they were little more
            than a dream.

        Each night,
        Hana sleeps dreamless.
        But behind her eyes
        isn't black.
            Green.
            Strong,
            dark,
            swirling . . .
        A tohu pushing its way out
            from inside
                  her womb.

Birth—Karaka

Walking through the snow
gun cocked on his shoulder
Matiu sees them rising
little particles of light
singing out   *We are here*
                and multiplying . . .
                We are here
                and rising.
He falls to his knees
as the particles
fill his lungs
to live in the caves
of his body.
They make their markings
deep in the dark.

Then he hears it,
like no song he has ever heard:
the threading of the child,
        into the rakatahi,
                into the kaumātua.
The voice of Hana's tāua
        threads through her mother's
                down into her own sacred call.

                        Kua whiria te aho tapu.
                        The karaka
                        has begun . . .

Birth—Hana

Her bare feet walk
towards the washing line.
The cold burns through
to the bone.
Then she hears it,
the soft high *tap*
of pounamu pieces
      gently touching.
      The high-pitched singing
      forged in tiny worlds of green.
      An opening
      for the rush of tides.
      Āhuru mōwai
      and her own voice
      add their harmonies.

She looks down at the snow
no longer white
      but pink and red.
She feels a vibration,
particles of light rising behind her eyes
moving out into her vision
to change the bloodied snow
                to green—
      a great lake
      expanding
      with a rim of snow
      at its edge.
            Lights flicker
            in spasms
            on the waves below.
      Creatures lurk
      beneath the ripples
      of ancient waka

moving across the circle,
        across this kōpae of potential.

A tiny shark thrashes,
pulling scaled prey apart
into flesh and red water.
A silent bird darts across the surface,
skimming the water
        with the edge of a wing.

Then she reaches for birthing posts
alone in the expanse.
Her hands fall
on snow.

Something whispers to her,
        E Hine, try again.
With the next rush she reaches
and feels a hand on each side.
        She sees them—
        somehow both shadow and light,
        absence of colour
        and all of it at once.

And as they hold her
she feels the currents
        move her body in its flux.
                She is the compass point
        as new directions
swim through her.

They are born to this world
        as she slips
        into the black.

Into
that dark dark
green.

Trouble

Running feet
through snow.

Matiu pushes through memories
of water crystallised
falling from sky to skin.

He sees her.

No, *them*.
Lying in a pool of red
as still as the whenua around them.

He runs to them,
puts the metal of his gun to her mouth,
sees her breath fog the steel.

She is alive.

He holds her,
screams
and shoots the sky.

Ko Rakinui e tū iho nei!
Send the village
to carry us home.

He hears them running
one million white crystals
stamped down with boots.
A village saves itself
again   and again   and again.

Aftermath

These babies are strange,
    the people said,
    for one was silent.
    More than silent,
    she was the absence of sound.
    The ringing in the ear after the muskets.
    A gramophone in reverse.

I heard that when their mother sings
one bub opens her mouth and swallows the song,
    the people said.
    Hana tried not to listen,
    their words like sandstone
    grating her away over years—
    a journey just beginning.

The other has never opened its eyes,
but when the doctors looked in them
all they saw was green,
    the people said.
    Not empty caves of sight
    in the face of Mahuika's fire.
    Pounamu orbs,
    like the goddess of death.
    The deep sight of stone
    that survives in the mind
    with less than light.

    And so the whānau turned inwards
    upon themselves,
    for maybe
    what the people said
            was true.

Naming Day

Homai kā mokopuna,
    Tāua Hinepūnui said,
    her long skirts flowing
    in the river where she stood.

Give me the quiet one first.
    The old woman
    held her moko
    to her chest,
    and sprinkled her
    with water from their awa.

You will be 'Te Heikiki',
    she said, as the water silently
    took its place in the river's flow.
A silent name, a gentle name, a beautiful name.
Like a bird in flight far above.
    And so all the sound of the water
    was pulled into the baby:
        Te Heikiki, the silent one.

Homai te pēpi tuarua,
    called the old woman.
    She took the one with greenstone eyes
    and let the water fall through the dark hair
    that crowned them.
You will be 'Reremai',
    she said, as the water became hands
    beckoning towards them.
For the look of the water in your eyes,
for the things you will call,
for the strength of the shark—
Reremai.

Then Matiu took all his mamae,
all his frustration and fear
and pushed his foot down on the shovel
to dig a hole big enough for their whenua,
their placenta and first sustenance.

He wrapped his hands around the neck
of a young rimu
and placed it in the soil.
      And so it was done.
      The children were born and named
                      in Waitaha.

Kōrero Tuatoru

In which Reremai and Te Heikiki have become rakatahi living with their māmā and pāpā at the back of a pā that often speaks ill of their ways and gifts, Te Heikiki's dreams are visited by a strange figure who leaves signs on her body of their meeting, Reremai finds a lover in a river and learns to channel their passion, and a suitor is arranged for Te Heikiki.

Kā Kaitapere

Players

Growth

The river is murky today
but the movement of eels
can be felt from the way
the waves flick up to meet my hands,
Te Heikiki whispers
inside the bones of Reremai.

Reremai exhales. *What else?*

Your breath is rising from your mouth
like licks of smoke from the chimney.
The wind moves the grass in sweeps.
It looks like the fabric from Māmā's dress
in the photo of her and Pāpā above the fireplace.

Reremai opens their eyes, dappled light flooding into the green.
And sister, how is our tree?

She is as tall as we are,
not yet blossoming,
but soon she will. She is twisted and strange.
                But Rere, she is strong.

Pāpā Comes Home

Reremai sits upon the hill.
>They hear his footsteps crush sunburnt grass.
A sound far and distant felt inside
from deep knowing, a familiarity of whakapapa.

>Inside the blackness
Reremai sees red threads spiralling out from their chest:
one for Māmā tracing back to the house,
one for Te Heikiki
out in a field dancing like the north wind,
and one for Matiu
that maps out the mountains,
hills, and rivers
he leaves in his wake.
Reremai sees his thread fraying.
The red dulls
to the colour of late summer roses,
the kind that grows far from here.

The crush of footsteps plays out
on the stage inside the mind:
*Pāpā is coming home
with his bag full
of stones.*

Carving

Matiu hands stones to Reremai, one by one.

Inaka, this one is light in colour, like white bait.

Rere feels the stone
smoothed by years of water
running over the stone fish trapped within.

Totoweka, the colour of the weka, with its blood splashing the stone.

Rere feels the feathers sticky,
trust broken with patu,
rustling and then still
under the cold surface.

*Kawakawa, the strongest and darkest stone, the embodiment
of Hinekawakawa . . . a rokoā, a medicine.*

Rere's hands warm over the stone.
Like immersing oneself in the pools of chiefs
where warm minerals swim through the water,
springing forth from cracks in the rocks.

And the most treasured from this journey. Putiputi, flower jade.

This is the one.
Rere cradles the stone—
flowers of gold bloom beneath the surface
at the summer warmth of Rere's hands.
A field of potential, with the form of a wahine swirling towards them.

Putiputi, a word too for a beautiful woman.

The woman opens her eyes to Reremai

in the mind's theatre,
a dark, dark green.
Subtly, unnoticed by all except
the hidden daughter of the mind,
the stone bends with Reremai's touch.

Stronger than steel,

Matiu says.

Stronger than steel.

Dancing

Everything here is a flat disc
and in the middle of this disc
surrounded by a witness of mountains
the world has a stage for a single dancer.
A swirling conductress of this island
shaped as an ancient canoe
with the children of the land
bending and swaying to her instruction.
The smallest wiri of the hands
a simple asking of Tāne Rore
to bring heat from his father, the sun,
from the ground
to move in waves
to the love
of the open sky.

She is speechless
in the western sense.
Her first reo the language of movement,
the language of muscle and bone.
So she spins   and spins   and spins
a tiny tornado of tūī in the winds around her
as she spirals them back to the highest heaven
to take her unspoken words home.

And in the distance
at the edges
something, or someone
in the caves
is listening
from every time they have existed
they prepare to join the dance
that they have waited for
since the song began.

Scene: The Bedroom of Matiu and Hana

H: *But Kiki can't be married—how will she ask for help if she can't speak? She should stay with me.*

M: *She has a better chance than Rere—they can't even see the stone they worship so much. Rere'll be sitting at that workbench touching those bloody stones until you put me in the ground.*

H: *But at least Rere speaks. Can say no—can scream for help.*

M: *Hana, we will have to find them good matches. Who knows for Reremai. Auē. It'll be hard to find matches to hold them down, who'll see them as just like anyone else.*

H: *Just like the others? Jesus, they're more than 'normal' Matiu, not less.*

M: *Hana, we're getting old. We have nothing to give them but this place, where we have to whisper in our room to protect them. Marae doesn't care because of what pā gossips say. They'll be stuck here until the house falls down around them. Is that what you want for your children?*

H: *None of this is what I wanted for them.*

***

M: *Hana, I will secure the future of our children. I will send them somewhere safe.*

Scene: The Bedroom of Te Heikiki and Reremai

R: *I want to be a carver, Kiki.*

K: *They'll never allow it. It's too dangerous. I know how the stone feels to you—it's like me when I'm dancing. It's like a marriage between you and the stone.*

R: *If you know how it feels how can you tell me it's wrong?*

K: *Because we're different, Rere. You see how the others treat us. They know how we speak, but do they speak with us? No. We're unwanted.*

R: *Suits me fine—if I'm a carver I'll have my own money. I'll go up the river for weeks at a time just like Pāpā. No one will notice me out there.*

K: *You won't be safe. And who will teach you if Pāpā won't? And don't act like you're the only one . . . no one can hear me but you. The only way I can speak is to move. How would you feel if you opened your mouth to scream and nothing came out?*

R: *I'd feel like I'd rather die than stop dancing. I'd find a way to dance.*

***

K: *Then you have to find a way to carve without cutting. You have to find another way to grind the stone down.*

Dreaming—Darkness to Light

A dark expanse of water
spreads across the eyeline
and then the song begins.
As it grows louder
the eyes begin to focus on colours,
shapes and the shadows they make on each other.
Soft warm air
moves the body
towards the centre of the dream.
Eyes flutter open
to the feel of
feathers and claws
guiding the body down
into the dark place of the water atua and who he touches.
Te Heikiki lets her body dangle
as this known stranger carries her
deep into the wave where sea and earth
become each other.
Takaroa—the ocean-made man.
Papatūānuku—the woman who holds us
safe upon her back.
Their celestial bodies
hold Te Heikiki and her winged angel,
her god-turned-ariā
as they flow
between each other
like a million hands
pulling at planetary flesh.

Then there is a breaking away,
the receding of water
that comes before a killing wave.
A new love forms,
pressing the two dreamers

between the mother they have learnt to love
and *Rakinui*, a new father in the sky.
Soon they are less alone
as more and more children emerge
to fill any gap.
These new gods
merge into each other,
into their parents,
while these hidden descendants
of an embrace eternal
hide as witnesses to the unfolding
of our beginning.

Until a speck of light trickles in,
a beacon of hope for more
than damp and pressure.

Then our dreamers' newfound siblings
try to push the sky away
only for it to fall on them again and again.
Until they hit peak confusion,
peak darkness.
This is how death and destruction
enter the world—
through sacrifice of a brother
who will never know the pleasure of light.

Then the heaving and hoeing,
the cutting and sawing,
as the blue blood of Rakinui,
pukepoto pigment,
soaks into the earth
with the red ochre blood,
the kōkōwai of Papatūānuku
and light floods the world
ki te ao mārama.

And through this timeless space
he is there
holding her, still.
The man with the feathers of rare birds
upon his arms
meets her eyes.
Inside those beady pools of black
Te Heikiki sees the beginning,
that big bang,
that pinprick of light showing what could be.
So she takes hands
mottled with the blood of the primordial father,
she places them on her body,
and the Artist begins
to draw.

Into the Black

Black is often misunderstood.
How often we say it is nothing,
a dark hole   an eater of light.
But black is so much more—
      all our dreams with the lights turned out,
      every cell before it was a cell,
      every colour in its earliest form.

And as we bring in the light,
as we remove the blindfold
we see black no more.
We see dark green,
      we see the true colour that comes
        when we look hard enough
            into the black.

Scene: The Bedroom of Matiu and Hana

H: *Matiu, are you . . . ?*
M: *Been awake all night*
H: *I thought as much—you're kicking like a swimmer*

***

H: *The house sounds different with you in it*
M: *Louder?*
H: *In a way. Like your mind keeps going*
     even when your body doesn't
M: *It feels that way, too. There's*
     so much to think about in this place
H: *You're allowed to stop for a while, you know?*
M: *But what if I stop holding everything and something falls?*
H: *Then I will catch it.*

***

M: *Will you catch me?*
     Hana?
     Will you catch me?
     Will you catch me, in your sleep?

Scene: The Bedroom of Te Heikiki and Reremai

*Sound: A draught moves in through the window
      as the sleepers hocket their breath*

* * *

Sound: A ruru calls in a tree filled with storm

*Sound: Two breaths become one as the air
      thickens with dreaming*

* * *

*Sound: One breath stops to breathe elsewhere.
      A sound of tapping. A sound of skin.
      A sound of overlap. Harmonies descend.
      A smell of blood. A sound of whakapapa.*

Pounamu

Reremai hears their tree
moving in the wind.
Inside them they see the veins of it
reaching to the sky,
twigs beckoning them to the river
like knowing hands.
The tiny sound of leaves
breaking from their homes
and landing as gentle ships on the awa.
Little pricks of percussion
on the rolling sound of water
as it moves towards the sea.

Underneath that white noise
there is a singing
so faint it could only be within the mind,
so faint it could only be an echo of a song long dead.
There is a lilting,
a sad weight to each beat.

Reaching into the liquid ice
the song bubbles upwards from the riverbed,
little pops of a voice
with the harmonies of a choir.
A voice older than stone
now trapped inside.
Reremai's shirt hits the bank,
their shoes long discarded
as they throw themselves into the water
listening for the song,
listening for the stone.

Light After Dreaming

Alone under wool blankets
Te Heikiki squeezes her eyes closed.
Imagines the bird-like man
hovering over her,
his breath on her face
like the winds of the beginning.
Imagines her eyelids held shut
by ancestors that appear
in shadows and low hums.

She opens her eyes to a dark room
with light leaking in.

Pounamu Kei Roto i te Awa

I hear you, I hear you, Reremai screams within as they thrash through the water, breath circling in their lungs as they become their own eco-system. The song blooms from a dark eddy across the river, deep under a bank. *I can hear you, I can hear you,* Rere assures as the water gets colder and darker and less like the life-giving liquid they have always trusted to cleanse and hold. The song is expanding. In fact, it is glowing. It is moving into Rere's cells, osmosis on the skin and in the eyes and ears. A golden sound pours over Rere, into every pore, except it is not golden—it's a brilliant green. Dark, dark, dark green. In the part of Rere that doesn't live amongst man, there is the tiniest crack of light. Then within the mind, Rere sees her—the pounamu woman lying under the water. Like Snow White in a liquid glass coffin. Except she is not to be rescued; she is ancient stone who travelled here from far away to escape. Rere reaches down into the water and when their hand touches the stone of her hair, it moves gently away from her face as if it isn't stone at all.

Marks

Kiki drags herself to her full height
as her nightdress lifts to show her thighs.
In the mirror she sees them—
a trajectory of long lines
ebbing and flowing
as pictures form
where the lines overlap.

Her thighs etched
tapped
painted
with a story of primordial lovers
woven together for eons
then breaking apart
so she could survive.

Touching

At this point in time,
Rere is only a picture
of what they have been taught to understand.
      Stone is sacred
      but still,   stationary,
      with a timescale far longer than that of man.
      Us humans with our fast movements,
      with generations spilling forth like water
      from an underground spring.

But now in these waters of potential
these āhuru mōwai,
stone is alive,
a pulsing thing that rises and falls.
Each breath within the lungs
building over centuries.
A time-lapse of one million years plays out
in Rere's calloused hands
as they touch the stone shape of a woman,
her green moving against their earthly skin
as if they are the river where they found each other.
Their epicentre   of themselves,
their centre   of the circle.

When they touch something stirs within Rere;
and when that feeling fills them completely
they open their eyes.
Hinepounamu gasps to see the worlds of stone
sheltered inside the bones
of this descendant of the land.
These pounamu spheres,
these worlds that contain nothing but kahere and moana.
      Nothing but seabeds and forest floors
      on which they may lie.

And in that moment light floods into Reremai.
No, not light,
for all but the stones is black velvet
wrapped around the consciousness.
      But within that soft darkness she is centred,
      a silhouetted brilliance of green,
      moko kauae chiselled by an even stronger stone.
      Delicate hair stronger than steel
      wraps around Rere's hands
            as it all slips away and they are there—
            the cursed child now grown
            and the woman made of stone
            learning how stone takes on the heat
            of Reremai's hands and body as they move upon her
            as she moves over them
            searching for the gentle pulsing
            of earthly blood
                  safe within the body.
                  Their kete of knowledge falls apart,
                  unravels to muka
                  ready for a new reality
                  to be woven.

Dreaming

Te Heikiki takes dream seconds to understand her position
on a battlefield where each moment lasts a century.
Where each blow of stone on stone shatters adzes to the wind.
Slow falling stone in air thick as water; stone warriors charge tectonic,
carving each other and cutting each other in fights that look like dances.
In a place where the elements are still dreamt of
a village of greenstone and a village of sandstone
fight each other across the earth.
At first it was a war; she and the Artist walked across the battlefield
completely unharmed as stone and sand maimed each other.
She removes her nightdress, the ghostly European sheath,
and lets it fly as Rona to the moon.
Hīnātore blossoms on the ceiling
like daisies dropped into black water
as Hoaka chases Pounamu across the world,
their flesh rubbing away with the sandy grit of their bodies.
The Artist is tossed into the contact points of this carving,
his toto the water to keep the cuts coming,
to make pounamu wet for the knife
but never hungry for the cutting.
Te Heikiki, with a full moon's strength
pulls him through to his descent, a flying shambles,
towards a cave where he collapses with her naked beside him.
Her Hineahuone skin, his Tāne Māhuta feathers and earth.
Over centuries of sleep-time she treats his wounds,
watches as people come through the cave.
The island is cut in by a giant of a man:
Rākaihautū lifts his kō, its tip
cut from the Pounamu on the run,
slices deep into the whenua,
primordial mother,
red with kōkōwai.
As pūrākau open out
like night-scented blooms

she notices
the golden skin,
the sharp *tī* and *tū*
of the bird-made man.
And so she calls
to the pou in the house,
to the drawings on the wall
asks, *Ko wai tōku tipuna?*
and they tell her to ask the eagle of a man
who flew down from the sky.
No need to ask what is known in the pito
as her body turns itself
through the small holes of the mind
and she becomes Hine-Nui-Te-Pō,
destined to be broken open by a grandson,
another who decides
to cheat a woman capable of death
and is crushed between the obsidian
of her legs.
He tara he waharoa
This is all a teaching
about the birth of death
while the physical form
begins its turning
for now she must return to life
for the first breath
of the son not yet earthside.

Awaken; Maniori

Around her body
the sheets are netted and knotted,
a fever shroud from when we Māori first got sick.
That first season of flu and famine
where the takiauē rolled out like fine gauze
        across this ship of a land.

    But inside this shroud
    is not a kind of sickness.
    It is a puawhānaka,
    a white flower that comes with the moonglow
    to tell us by blossoming
    within wet darkness
    that new life
    has begun.

    Underneath the fabric
    on top of skin just woken,
    the paintings of the Artist
    thread lines of fresh-cut rivers
    kōkōwai and oil
    over her abdomen,
    down and out
    and through to the ocean
    we were fished from.
    The awa atua running free,
            te pae o Tiki,
            open.

Carving

At first, Rere's stage is blank. The empty hall of the mind, the potential of performance. *Te Korekore.* Then a map, a blueprint, traces its lines for feet to follow. *Map maker, map maker,* found in the way the body remembers. Found in the way the body listens for distance, in the way the body knows it is not alone in the universe. Yet Rere waits for the knowing they are alone in this house. When the guest of stillness arrives, Rere moves through the map to Matiu's shed, heart pounding. The stones inside sing songs heard only in the mind, that colour the blackness inside. *I hear you, I hear you.* Rere opens the door and feels their presence. A warmth, a trapped fire; *their mauri.* The piece for this taoka calls. *I hear you, I hear you,* Rere whispers with the mind, with the body and its histories. Matiu enters the mind's stage, wading through a river all sunburnt and wild: *Nature always tells you what she wants.* Tonight it is a toki. Simple, sleek, but dignified and strong. Like Matiu himself, a man shaped by these elements, buffed into timely softness by the Southern winds. Rere turns on the water and feels the flow, cold and cleansing. Remembering the sounds, and knowing the feel of these tools, they let the chisels take centre stage as they begin to shape the stone. In their element, an artist bringing through what they have already seen deep within themselves, within the stone, and within that black stage of potential, *Te Korekore.*

Friction

Tuatahi

Reremai's heart pounds
Ta, ta-ta, ta-ta, ta-ta . . .
Running over paths they've known so long
guided softly by the sound of the song
Ta, ta-ta, ta-ta, ta-ta . . .
To the riverbed, to the riverbed
on which to rest and lay your head
Ta, ta-ta, ta-ta, ta-ta . . .
Where the greenstone woman lies
in tears of Aoraki as he cries
Ta, ta-ta, ta-ta, ta-ta . . .
Where the sting of cold is nothing compared
to her green skin and pounamu hair
Ta, ta-ta, ta-ta, ta-ta . . .
Arriving at the sharp sting of water
cross the currents to the stone daughter
Ta, ta-ta, ta-ta, ta-ta . . .
With a taoka at your chest
a new koha to adorn her breast
Ta, ta-ta, ta-ta, ta-ta . . .
Ta, ta-ta, ta-ta, ta-ta . . .
Pounding, pounding like white water on stone
Ta, ta-ta, ta-ta, ta-ta . . .
You touch her and feel electric
a song in your bones
Ta, ta-ta, ta-ta, ta-ta . . .
Ta, ta-ta, ta-ta, ta-ta . . .
Ta, ta-ta, ta-ta, ta-ta, ta-ta

Tuarua

Touching again,
Hinepounamu and Rere.
The slippery smooth of the stone
like shark skin from her lands far away.
As if this person is already part of her,
as if they are moulded from her
like a rib from Adam
except they are both complete without the other.
Rere made part of a wider spectrum of seeing
from these spheres of stone.

She thinks of the ancient one she saw
hovering over the stone corpses of the dead,
Hine-Nui-Te-Pō with eyes the dark green of her flesh.
But that was different:
a possession, an ownership,
so different to her whaiāipo,
who she would reach for
in the darkness
found only in water
beneath a Whiro moon,
only to find nothing
but the resistance
of the mountain's tears.

Tuatoru

Clutching each other
like pearls,
like pounamu,
they lie together in the shallows.
Water on stone
softening her curves over centuries,
puckering Reremai's skin.
In the stillness
Rere opens the buttons of their shirt
revealing a hei tiki—
rough, but clear as to its purpose.
Waha shaped, an infinity filled in
with more of itself.
Thoughts race as she gasps.
Did they find this for her?
Reremai puffs their chest,
proud kererū love drunk and dumb.
I carved it for you myself.
The air suddenly becomes so thin
that love can fall through it,
can break like a stone
from a great height.

Tuawhā

Hinepounamu shakes
holding the scarred talisman.
The marks of hōaka, sandstone,
still visible at its edges.
The reshaping of one thousand cuts.
Not death, but a worse fate—
a removal of identity,
a shaping and division of cells.
How could you, how could you.
Rere is confused;
this was the most beautiful action
they could take for her,
they could make for her,
they could make *of* her . . .
And then Rere sees them,
the cuts on Hine's body
peeking through the stone piupiu,
gaps in her legs and arms,
her chest full of valleys
like lush ravines.
And then they know
the deed they have done
not out of love
but out of haste.

Tuarima

They lie together in shock and hate
warmth changing to cold
until finally the ice breaks
with the sea change of tears.
Drops of warm ocean
mingle between them,
an estuary between land and sea.
Pounamu piu
clack and slide,
stage curtains opening
to reveal a ledger of the past on the body.

Her stone tears hang in the water,
pearls of the stream
coming to rest on a bed of mud and gravel.
Rere holds her
as she lets them fall.

As they part in forgiveness
nimble stone fingers pick up her tear drops.
Kā roimata, she says.
There must be a better way,
as she drops the tears into Rere's open palm
like the rain from Raki for Papa.
She closes Rere's hand over the pile of green jewels.
Maybe there's a way in here,
in these.

Tuaono

Inside the dark velvet of Reremai's mind
stone tears pool in outstretched hands.
A meditation on each release,
of Hinemoana, Hinemokemoke
crying from inside the body.
Except their whaiāipo is all stone,
from the pūmotomoto down into the riverbed.

Reremai thinks deep into the stone,
deep into its centre,
and then focuses deeper still.
The distillation of green
blurring and shaking.
A shift in focus
vibrating below eye level;
Kōhatu mauri ora!

They let their thoughts travel
to the form of the hei tiki,
the guardian of te pae o Tiki.
They let their thoughts travel to their sister
and all the weight that being a woman has pressed down upon her.
They think of how Kiki sneaks around the house
like a little cat,
covering herself with her Sunday skirts
all days of the week.
Arms shawl-wrapped
as she swirls in the landscape,
eyes closed,
hands outstretched
to whatever lies beyond the sky.
Reremai pictures her,

a film they watch through pounamu spheres.
Projections of the world
play over and through the teardrops
cradled in Reremai's palm.

Then all of that focus
all of that aro
all of that hā
moves
like sun rays
unseen
into the hidden stones.
And when Reremai
opens their hand
a hei tiki
freshly born
lies there,
its arms and legs etched
with something unexpected.
But on the face the markings are deep
and suddenly
Reremai feels more
than they may ever understand.

Reveal

Rere runs to their beloved
Ta, ta-ta, ta-ta, ta-ta . . .
the new hei tiki gripped in the hands
till their knuckles turn white
Ta, ta-ta, ta-ta, ta-ta . . .
Today they will show how they can adapt,
change, create, grow,
assimilate with the whānau of their lover
Ta, ta-ta, ta-ta, ta-ta . . .
A way they can be useful,
a way they can learn to bend and not break
Ta, ta-ta, ta-ta, ta-ta . . .

Into the water Rere goes,
across the wet highway
to Hinepounamu.
I have something I made for you.
They open their hand to reveal
the hei tiki.
Mottled kawakawa pounamu with aotea,
totoweka, putiputi: a creation that exists only
through the magic
living in the minds of the twins.
From your tears,
a talisman of the future,
the guardian of the birth canal,
the first man.

She takes it and hears
the little clack
of stone on stone,
the tiniest song of tumutumu rhythm.
No, that's not all of what this is.

Rere thinks back
to Kiki dancing lost, covered in cloth
with colour sifting through the fine fibres.
This is your sister and who she has become.

Rere's breath quickens
Ta, ta-ta, ta-ta, ta-ta . . .
You must go to her,
and ask her what she has done
Ta, ta-ta, ta-ta, ta-ta . . .
She too has secrets
that fall deep below this earth
and far above.
Hine takes Rere's finger
to stroke the taoka
sitting safe within her hand;
See, look what you have discovered!
And there beneath the firm lines
gracing the pito of the hei tiki,
something moves,
and kicks gently,
a tiny footprint
within
the stone.

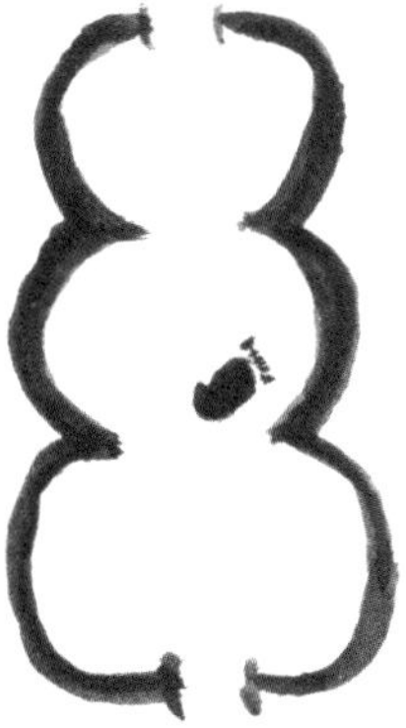

Scene: The Bedroom of Matiu and Hana

M: *He's the perfect man for Kiki, Hana—respected on the pā, two children from a previous marriage. Needs a woman around.*

H: *There's no such thing as a perfect man. How will he treat her when she doesn't speak? What if her children suffer the same fate as she has? Each day she grows more detached. More wairua than tinana, more fairy than woman, and you think she's ready to create a family with some man who's desperate to latch onto our whakapapa?*

M: *It's not like that at all. He's gentle, trusted. She deserves that security—to have what we have, with her own family. She deserves to be more than a mute end to the whakapapa you want to protect her from.*

H: *Well at the end of the day, it's not for me to say—it's for her to tell you. You need to talk with her, like you would with Reremai.*

M: *Haven't you seen me trying? Haven't you seen me holding her hand and talking her through this world every day of her childhood? Can't you see that I'm doing all this for her?*

H: *You talk at her, Matiu. You don't talk with her. You're not doing this for her—you're doing this for your seat on the paepae. For how the bloody marae see you. You're doing this for a club of men who will be dead long before our daughter, and you're doing this for yourself.*

M: *You're all too stubborn—you, Rere, and your daughter. Come Monday, I'm taking her to meet George Ihupuni and that's that. If you want to help, you can talk to her about what it means to be a wife—if you even know.*

H: *I'll talk to her, but don't you forget. You may be a man, but you are not a rakatira, you are not a chief.*

Scene: The Bedroom of Te Heikiki and Reremai

R: *I saw what's been happening, inside my head. I saw a man who's blurred . . .*

K: *Whatever you think you saw, you won't understand. It's harmless, he's just a dream that I have now and then. He takes me places, shows me things only our old people's old people could have seen, and Rere—no part of me is willing to give that up.*

R: *I'm not telling you to give him up. But what I saw there was something . . . permanent about it. Something that went below the surface. In the stones, in the cord between us . . .*

K: *It's not your job to worry about me. There's no pressure on you to do well, get married. That's what's been given to me and I'm being forced to take it. But until I do, I'm my own person.*

R: *All I know of you now is how little you let me in.*

K: *Well, what about you? Coming home at all hours soaking wet, the anger, the secrecy. How would you feel if I stopped listening to you when you called? Sometimes I tug and tug at that line between us and nothing moves. You're jealous. You want me helpless and all to yourself just like everyone else. But I never will be. No matter what Māmā and Pāpā do, I won't go.*

R: *All I said is that you've been distant—I was worried. But I've seen the marks in the stone. I know you're hiding them under your skirts, and I know what else you're hiding. I don't think any new husband will be happy about it.*

K: *Well, if you spend all your time in the water, you'll drown eventually. Is that what you want? Is whatever is calling you really worth it?*

Kōrero Tuawhā

In which Te Heikiki is promised to a proud man of the pā, Reremai builds Hinepounamu a home from the remnants of her pain, Te Heikiki is exposed, Māmā takes charge, Reremai shares their gifts, and a new babe is born.

Kā Kaitapere

Players

Hana

Hinepounamu

Reremai

Matiu

The A... ...ikiki

Aurumea

George Ihupani

She Is Betrothed

Pāpā tells her to put on her best dress. Pāpā tells her brush her hair. Pāpā tells her there will be children. She has always liked children. Pāpā tells her to wear the taoka he made for her 18th birthday, the hei tiki in blue aotea. Nothing less for a stone carver's daughter. *Wear it draping down*, he tells her, *not sidewise—that's not the message we want to send.* She unhooks the loop she made to hold it horizontal; the position that shows she is finished with bearing children, Pāpā tells her, though she already knows. Pāpā tells her to put her good shoes on. Kiki swirls around in her Sunday best. Māmā says nothing, but thinks how like a child she is when she dances. Grabs her hand, looks into her eyes, and squeezes the fingers gently into the palm.

Pāpā leads her out beyond the gate. Pāpā leads her to the middle of the dirt road. Pāpā leads her away from her home as the people of the pā peep through their windows, whispering. *That's the strange one, the 'dancer'. Always been odd, and the other one is practically a hermit.* Pāpā leads her out into the main street. Pāpā leads her past the windows of the big houses. *Look, they're doing something! The one who steals stone and that quiet girl of his.* Pāpā leads her away to a villa on the corner. Tidy, modest, a carving at the doorway with pūkana blaring a challenge. Pāpā knocks.

A nanny answers, welcomes Pāpā. Welcomes Kiki. Pāpā leads her inside to a room with a fire and toys. There are two children, a boy and a girl. They look up at Kiki like ruru in the daytime. Pāpā tells her to sit down. She places herself on the floor with them, plays silent music on their xylophone, pushes a small fire truck towards them under the table. Soon they are laughing, though it can be seen only in the shaking of their bodies, the air moving in and out. The room is warm and feels like it is the first day of a new spring blooming, tiny petals folding out and smoothing their creases.

Pāpā looks to the doorway shadowed by a man closer to his age than his daughter's. George Ihupuni. *Get up and greet Mr Ihupuni, Kiki,* Pāpā says. She rises to her full height and meets his gaze. He is holding the house up around him, like he is the ridgepole and the children are safe in the space underneath him that will never grow taller to fit. He smiles kindly. *It's lovely to meet you, e te putiputi, wonderful to have you here in our home.* Pāpā is sweating through his shirt. He leads himself towards the door as Mr Ihupuni steps forward to Kiki. *I've been looking forward to our little visit.*

Becoming Accustomed

Kiki walks to the house of George and the children
every Friday night and Sunday morning.
There is comfort to the routine,
like waiting for the second hand
to move on a clock
then adding up the minutes
until the chime of the hour motivates you
to wait again
and count the seconds
you know will pass.

She plays with the children
and they learn from her silent ways,
moving their lips in empty motions,
giggling as if underwater.
While their mother's portrait
rules over them
from the mantel
he watches
the developing potential
of her replacement
as she plays string games
with their children:
cup and saucer,
witch's hat
and cat's cradle.
He licks his lips.

He is always polite.
When they sit down for a meal,
she eats first.
He waits for her to take her first bite
and then begins himself
to slice at the meat.

Discovery

The room is dimly lit,
the children long asleep.
Her breath pools in her chest
as his eyes survey
her earthen skin,
her korowai of hair.
Is it ok if I . . .
She freezes, her blood turned to stone.
Then she screams in her head,
Reremai! Reremai!
His breath becomes the only sound,
his hands moving to her buttons,
fumbling as the stone of her blood
moves into her muscles,
into her mind.
But still
she pictures that aho,
that sacred line
and she tugs it with all her strength.
Reremai, please . . .
But Rere is not there.
And as the fingers remove her clothes
something switches within the room.

The ochre fades from the wood.
The air runs cold.

He gasps as he hesitantly touches
fresh moko on her skin,
the Artist's signature.
The air grows colder still
as he moves down.
Placing hands across her hips,
he sees the rise of flesh

beneath the painted canvas
of her skin.
His blood flushes his cheeks.
An assumed ownership, thwarted
by the weight of a child in wānanga
within his virginal bride.

He calmly stands
and leaves the room
taking the light and air
with him.

He Pā Pounamu

Hinepounamu nuzzles her lover's neck
its warmth moving into the stone.
These people of blood, tears, and decay.
Of love, of taoka, of familial ties,
just like her.

It's been over a month
since she showed Reremai
her greatest taoka
and her most painful memory.
The broken pounamu waka
and its long dead crew
strewn upon the riverbed.
Rere held her
as she cried small stones
over the wreckage.

And from that wreckage
Reremai set to work
using their hands,
their focus,
their aro and hā
to reshape these artifacts of the past
into a microcosm of paradise
to surround her.
A pounamu pā on the riverbed
where she could live
rather than just survive in the shallows.
A raupō roundhouse moulded from finest kawakawa stone
with a riverbed garden and deep green flax planted inside the tūwatawata,
the stone fence cleverly carved
from the oars of the great canoe.
A stone tūī ringing with life,
singing underwater

sipping
on stone nectar.

Hinepounamu strokes Rere's hair as they sleep
on the riverbank
appearing as any other couple
lying together by a rimu under the full moon.
Rere's body tenses in sleep
their breath heavy and fast,
branches moving above them
in an unseen wind.
Reremai . . . Reremai . . .
Pounamu spheres open to the moon.
I have to go, she's in trouble.
And all the while
the tūī calls a wet warning.
But nobody hears it
at all.

Exposure

This is how she learns
that he is not a kind man.
        Her skirt in her arms,
        and her shirt wrapped around her,
        she moves forward on the dirt road.
        The patterns of her body
        appear otherworldly—
        neither ancient nor modern
        but present.
        A ghostly kind of physicality,
        onāianei—*of this moment*
        made flesh
        to the folk
        who peek through windows
        as she is marched from the top street
        down to the lowest.

He pushes her through the gate
as women and children
gossip under the awnings.
The moon a stage light
for the audience to her body.
        Curse you,
she calls in silence to the moon.
        Curse you.

With his three bangs on the door
her mother and father
appear like pou before her.
Your daughter is either crazy, cursed,
or both. He mākutu. All of you. Cursed.

Kiki is pushed into her mother's arms.
Maiden and mother,

standing on the verge of
mother and crone.

As Reremai arrives from the kisses of the river,
George Ihupuni pushes past them
on his way back
to the good part of the pā.

Clean

Māmā tells her to head inside. Māmā heats up water, swirls soap through like a potion, round and round. Māmā puts towels by the fire to warm. Māmā puts kawakawa, honey, sliced apple, and water into a pot on the stove. Te Heikiki sits by the fire, her eyes staring beyond the world in front of her. Māmā fetches the water and tea. When she returns Kiki has not moved. The pictures across her body are ancient in the firelight, like birthmarks rather than scars. Moko rather than tattoo. *There's no worries, bub, let's get you sorted first. Bed tonight, everything else can wait. You're home now.* Māmā takes a flannel and gently soaps Kiki. She traces the lines from her thigh up to her chest, then down to the swell of her abdomen where the marks of te awa atua, the river of gods, now flows around her, protecting the wahi tapu within. She begins to recognise the patterns. Marks from her childhood cave, that sacred place where she and Matiu found each other. Māmā feels her heart race, *ta, ta-ta, ta-ta, ta-ta . . .*

Did Matiu and I sign some otherworldly contract as we lay under the drawings of our tīpuna? Did I set my children on a course where all they were destined for was silence, darkness, and pain? Her thoughts fall like stones down her throat and into her chest. Māmā dries Kiki off, then wraps her in a blanket. She sees how she had looked as a small child, fresh from the river. Matiu would play with them for hours making dams and eeling in the winter, swimming and telling stories on the bank during summer. She had tried to give them all a good life despite the obstacles raining down upon them like adzes, nicking their skin and cluttering their path. Māmā retrieves a night gown, hair brush, oil, and a mug of the wairākau for each of them. Kiki moves at last to slowly sip the warmth. Māmā straightens her hair out over the blanket, Kiki's hair dark with red flecks like vines upon the pastel wool. She moves oil through the thick locks, and brushes gently, mana restoring for her girl, flesh of her flesh. She sends this love through her fingertips, avoiding where her fontanel was once open for other worlds to drift in and out. Maybe they are still drifting. Maybe Kiki knows more than she could ever say.

Māmā feels how she used to feel while she was waiting for the twins to be born, a song building within her, each movement a rhythm, each feeling a note. The longer she listens, the more the raki allows itself to form. Māmā begins to hum the tune that is circulating around her body, her daughter beginning to sway as the humming grows. She knows then what it is. An oriori. A song for a baby before it comes into te ao mārama, their world of light. Māmā listens deeply to the notes above and below her that are growing out from inside the tune. *Irirangi*, she was told in her girlhood days by her own mother, who had been told the same from her mother— just in a different language then. *Your voice is special because inside it is the voices of our ancestors, the spirit voices, the irirangi.* Her tāua passed when the children were still small, and her mother too as they grew older, almost cutting her and her strange family off from their people completely. She sings now, round open tones with the high echoes reaching through the past to sing their parts. She feels Kiki relax as she pulls the nightgown over her head, while the sound of a kōauau plays somewhere in the distance; she swears she can hear it. *Go on to bed now. We'll talk in the morning.* Kiki rises and holds her māmā, her full height still not that of the previous generation, with the ones before looming larger still in their minds. They hold each other. Outside, Reremai plays kōauau. Its pounamu was repurposed from the tears of their beloved, from the hei tiki that was meant to protect their sister, but never reached its true owner. Changed now to help their whānau to cry, changed now to give them all voice.

Scene: The Bedroom of Matiu and Hana

H: *They're both settled now, at last. This is something we could be dealing with for years, Matiu. I hope you're happy.*

M: *Of course I'm not happy . . . I thought we had it all figured out.*

H: *We? No, you had it all figured out. How to mask them, our beautiful babies. They have gifts, Matiu! They could have lived here together all their lives. But you had to go and tell them what they could and couldn't do. Just as your family did with you.*

M: *Look, I'm not proud of what I've done. If I'd known, I would have left them to figure themselves out. I just thought this would be better . . . for all of us.*

H: *Well, heaven knows what the pā thinks of us all now . . . and it's Kiki I feel sorry for.*

M: *I just wanted the best for our children, and do you blame me? Do you blame me for worrying what people would do to them? Kiki was stripped half naked and paraded down the street, for god's sake!*

H: *That's nothing compared to what's been done to her body. Was that from this 'perfect' man you sold to us, nē?*

M: *I saw too. If it's George's he'll be paying.*

H: *It doesn't matter whose it is. It's Kiki's so it's whānau. And we will behave accordingly—understand?*

M: *Yes, of course.*

H: *Good.*

Scene: The Bedroom of Te Heikiki and Reremai

R: *I came as soon as I heard you. I'm so sorry. I thought you had everything under control.*

K: *I was just doing my best with what I was given, and I understand now, that wasn't a lot.*

R: *You've done fine. It's not like people around here expected any more of us anyway. Just tell me what you need and I'll sort it, and there's someone I want you to meet, when this is all over.*

K: *When this is all over? Do you really think this will ever be all over for me? I'm a marked woman, Rere—inside me there is a child who has monsters for parents. And my skin—*

R: *But what if we're not monsters? What if we're more than human? What if we're touched by the atua themselves, I know I—*

K: *But are there any risks for you? Do people try to marry you off like some silent status symbol? No, they don't. But you wouldn't have thought about that would you, Rere?*

R: *Look, I'm not the one you need to fight. If you need me now, you've got me. If you don't, well . . . just tell me. But I want to be here, and I want you to meet her.*

K: *The pounamu woman? Yeah, I've seen you two. We're linked Rere—no secrets even if we tried. But you haven't been looking, you haven't seen him, the artist I see at night, his wings, where we go . . . it's like the world I was supposed to be in.*

R: *Rather than the one we got?*

K: *Yes exactly—it's like the world we deserve.*

Dreaming—Reunited

It has been a long time
since her love has lifted her wairua
from her body, within the dreaming.
But as soon as she enters that dark space
like silk swimming in water,
as soon as she smells the kōkōwai and oil,
she knows he is here.
She closes her eyes, feels feather and warmth
before opening them to find
the Artist.
She sees his body—
thinner,
slightly beaten,
and understands that even immortal men
suffer time and punishment.
When she rises up before him,
he looks distraughtly at her body,
centre stage within this envelope of blackness.
He moves over the moko,
healing now in black and red.
Down to her abdomen etched
with the markings of the awa atua
now bursting its banks.

He opens his arms wide
as the blackness slips away,
a curtain rising
to reveal twelve heavens of sky
going up   and up   and up.
She grips her arms around his neck,
her head pressed to his chest
as he soars upwards
in the open air.
Kā hau e whā

swirl as one where their bodies meet,
their resistance pushing them ever upward,
his arms feathered and flying
as they shield her
like a stitchless korowai.
But soon her arms begin to slip.
First the tension of holding too much
then the slipping of not enough
but he does not notice.
It is as if he is trying to reach Aukumea,
the heaven where the unborn souls wait.
To reach in and retrieve his child himself
while its mother clings to life
far above the lands that bore them both.

Aukumea

It is hard to explain to you what this place is
without the senses that you had before your birth.
The higher understanding of a place where souls swim
not in water, but in sound.
I am a lucky one
who remembers how to swim
upon the irirangi
upon the rhythmic taps of our earthen mother.
In this space I learnt all things,
only to be robbed of language
but I do not need language to sing,
I do not need language to feel.
The eyes and the soul are formed together in utero
and I have felt myself sinking since then.
Harmonics fall to notes that shake me
from inside out.
Hearing all, with all I have.
My skin feels the music;
my soul sings.
And now as this space fades from me,
Father is here
and it is time to go.

Fever Dreaming

Heavy breathing pierces the darkness.
Reremai awakes with the tugging of the cord,
the sacred thread woven through time.
They move towards Te Heikiki's bedside,
following the sound of tiny storms in the lungs.
>*Stop*, Māmā whispers
>*Never wake someone in this kind of dream*

Reremai freezes.
>*What kind of dream is that, Māmā?*

They hear her hands winding a porotiti
to blow fresh air over Kiki's face,
damp with sweat.
>*The kind where you go somewhere*
>*to bring something back . . .*
>*The kind where there's a risk*
>*you might accidentally*
>*leave yourself behind.*

Dreaming—Transformation

Higher and higher they go
as more and more feathers
grow to cover
the bird-like man
the winds continuing to push them
up and up and up.
As she starts to slip
she feels him speak to her.
You have to change, you have to adapt.
She clings to him.
How? How do I change myself?
This is all I am.
They are so high now
that looking down
Kiki sees nothing but a disc world
of water and sand,
with their Southern waka
lying dormant beneath.
You are a daughter of Hineahuone
and you are a daughter of Hinepūnui-o-Toka.
Use the winds to shape the clay of your body.
And then she understands.
She lets herself go
as soil and water,
as earth
shaped into flying beast.
A bird-like woman
sung into being
by the winds
of the South.

Dreaming—Weaving

Reremai awakes again
to find their mind silent,
alone with the black hills
of the mind's eye.
Kiki, Kiki . . .
they whisper inside themselves
before moving towards the bed.

> *No, don't touch. She still sleeps,*
Māmā says, vigilant by her bedside
with her spinning disc and strange singing
that bubbles up through the air in her body
to ring out inside the head.
> *I don't know what's happening now,*
> *but I hope she hears me . . .*
> *I hope she hears the song*
> *and follows it through*
> *towards the world of light.*

Reremai feels empty:
empty handed,
empty minded.
As if any skill that may help Kiki
has dried up
within the riverbed of their body.

But empty hands may still work,
so they run to the river.
Ta, ta-ta, ta-ta, ta-ta . . .
to the riverbed home of their beloved
Ta, ta-ta, ta-ta, ta-ta . . .
where they share the story of this silent sister,
from one set of pounamu eyes
to another.

Rere asks for permission,
then cuts the stone flax.
Only the grandmother leaves
to protect the rito,
the baby sheltered by whakapapa
on the inside.

Running back to Māmā now
Ta, ta-ta, ta-ta, ta-ta . . .
Their secrets about to be spoiled
Ta, ta-ta, ta-ta, ta-ta . . .

Māmā and Pāpā sit in silence
over a girl so still she could be made of clay.
Māmā, I need you to show me what to do.
I want to weave a wahakura for the baby.

A mist of shock settles upon the room
like a fine dusting of glass.
The silence of one twin locked in a dream
and the other with leaves of ancient stone
            is deafening.
            Yes, of course I'll help you.
Māmā breaks the glass
            Sit here on the floor, and I'll tell you,
            but you'll have to do the work.
            You're the only one who can weave the stone.

And with that the family is together
sitting in wānaka,
preparing for something long ago dreamt of
that may or may not arrive.
Pāpā's eyes are tainted
with a pride he knows
he does not deserve

as the best carver
the pā has ever seen
          is made before him.

Dreaming—Birth

Tuatahi

For the first time together
they soar
over the caves where they sheltered,
over the strings of mountains that were once mighty waka
or brothers trapped by karakia lost mid-recitation.
They soar and spiral together on and on and on,
circling downwards by the sea to weep;
weep for the snippets of life they may steal together,
weep for the traditions of storytelling and symbols
etched upon their bodies.
The tears of the albatross
fall down,
stitching longing
deep into the skin like tukutuku
as birds screech and scramble above.
Birds of land and sea
fight over the richness of rivers,
a great war filling the skies
to signal an imminent birth.
Together they fly to safety:
a cave nest
tucked away
from feather and blood.

Exhausted they collapse
in layered circles of sticks,
feathers and down.
She feels herself weighted low,
moving around their nest.
This new life as bird wife
with limbs too vast,
and body too taut.

Pain inside her
soon becomes too much
for bird to bear
and that is when
the black silk of darkness
returns.

Tuarua

She finds herself in her own form of flesh,
curled in their nest
around a clay egg.
Her body aches as she rolls herself to sit
and finds the Artist at work,
his horoeka paintbrushes dripping kōkōwai
as he paints his son on the wall,
a bird embryo held safe
in an egg.

He realises she has woken
and goes to hold her,
his inked hands marking her arms and face.
Gently he lifts the egg to his chest,
cradles it
like any doting Māori pāpā
and he says the words
Me whakaira takata
and the egg cracks
to reveal
a world of light.

Arrival

Te Heikiki opens her eyes
not to a cave,
but to a ceiling,
to a fire crackling in the other room.
To the smell of soap and water,
the sounds of breath rising.
She's awake, Māmā, she's awake!

She sees Reremai, Māmā and Pāpā
in chairs around the bed,
the late sun turning them sepia
in the small room.
      Baby, look what you've done.
      Look how clever you are.

And there next to her
in a beautiful wahakura
is the child of her and the Artist,
woven together across worlds.

      She lifts him from this taoka,
      this kaitiaki of sleep and dreams,
      and when he cries
      it sounds like the whole world
            is singing.

Kōrero Whakanoa

In which three years have passed, life has settled, and it is time for celebration.

Kā Kaitapere

Players

Down by the river
time flows out
like a ribbon.
Te Heikiki is gathering her thoughts,
small crystals of knowing
that she places inside herself.
Reremai's kōauau,
a gift from them and Hinepounamu
who today lies below the shallow waves
tending a garden of pounamu hue
and putiputi.

She pushes her hā through the instrument,
a thin note spreading
out into the air.
It feels strange after being silent for so long.
She still speaks to the world
in all the ways she has learnt how.
For her, this is how the world
will speak back.

A voice joins her kōauau
as if from another room.
A toddler
stands on the riverbank
painting the stone wall,
their eyes wild with focus,
the song leaking from their lips.
Though they cannot hear
outside of themselves,
their body has the great acoustic
of a chapel
except wild found—
a grand cave filled with paintings
as songs vibrate the walls
to life.

They named the baby Aukumea
for the heaven he was retrieved from,
for the paradise of men before they become men.
He sings knowing that his mother plays to him;
though he cannot hear her musings,
he feels them, as pinpricks of light
rising from under the skin.
His world is one of silence
filled with song.

Aukumea stretches out blue-dyed hands
to the stone bank before him
pukepoto, the sacred blue earth
his paint of choice.
He comes from a long line of cave painters,
a long line of artists
that loops back upon itself.
      Like the rivers
           his ancestors painted,
     like the tattooed lines
             on the body.

The kōauau song travels on the wind
to Reremai as they walk upstream,
their dry clothes sticking
to their still-damp body.
The scent of river water
nestles in their collarbones
and the strands of their hair.

They follow the sound
to find Te Heikiki, somehow more quiet
than she was before she could create sound.
Aukumea, their nephew, painting the bank,
     mouth wide open
       with the voices of an ancestral choir

spilling forth
  like rain after drought.
It's almost time, Kiki,
they say in their own secret way.

She wades across the river to the baby.
What are you painting, e te tau?
Aukumea says nothing, just hurries along
to finish before the big ceremony.
Show me what you've made.

It is two figures back-to-back
with a smaller one between them,
together forming a larger entity
that looks forwards, backwards,
  out, and in.
  Pāpā is behind,
Aukumea says, back in this place at last.

  It's beautiful, my clever son,
  Kiki says, gathering her blue-stained boy
  in her arms.
  Come on, it's time.

***

When she arrives,
the women have already gathered in the main room.
The fireplace is lit, the room immaculate
thanks to Māmā.
Blankets and a pillow are laid out for her,
with the kaitaka, the finest cloak from the pā,
which will protect her on this journey,
hung upon the wall,

ready to lie across her sleeping body.

She walks past Pāpā in the kitchen
preparing food and tea.
His face lights up
when he sees the twins and the boy.
      Big day, eh?
He embraces them all,
never saying he is proud
but showing it all the same.

They move into the room
where Māmā and all the aunties are waiting;
      Are you ready to go?
Māmā asks, beaming her anticipation.
Kiki nods.

She lies down upon the blankets
and the kaitaka,
the weight of ten thousand stitches
is laid upon her,
holding her steady.

      Mā wai te karakia?
      Māmā asks

Reremai looks around the room,
seeing their mother with two extra shadows
one like their grandmother, and one whose hair
blows in an impossible Southern breeze.

      Māku
      Reremai responds, eager and ready.
      Unuhia, unuhia . . .

138

Kiki looks around at her whānau.
They've learnt to understand each other,
they've learnt to see her and her twin
and the baby as crucial parts of the pā:
as messengers, historians, as artists.
    Tihei . . .
    Mauri ora,
    they all reply.

She takes a last look at her son
Aukumea,
one of the many places
she has travelled so far with her beloved.
Each time, her skills have become stronger and stronger.
And today she will take her moko kauae.
She doesn't need to ask
what her lover will paint for her;
she saw it on the cave wall:

    Two twins back-to-back,
    her baby in the centre,
    her whaiāipo at the back,
    all of them gazing in different directions
    to together see the world
    how it was always meant to be seen . . .

Aukumea
begins to sing
in an enchanted voice
made of multitudes:
the irirangi, the irewaru,
the voices of the wind sisters too
singing within the celestial choir
distilled down to just one thread.

She closes her eyes
as her mother and sibling
take her hands
and she begins again
to dream her way
into the black silk
of the beginning,
Reremai playing

and her son

Aukumea

singing her

into being.

Mihi

Kā mihi nunui ki ōku tīpuna; ko koutou te puna hōhonu o pūrākau. I am lucky to be able to swim in your stories and emerge anew. Thanks to Fergus and the team at Te Herenga Waka University Press with special mention to Jasmine for her care with these words and characters, thank you for treating them as the written descendants of whakapapa that they are. We are all very grateful for your aroha and guidance. To my partner, Daniela, who tolerated the many sticks, stones, and bones that filled our house during the writing of this mahi aroha; thank you for letting me live in so many worlds at once and always being there to welcome me home to yours.

Tēnā koe, Ihāia Ryan, for helping to shape these characters, and gifting Matiu, Hana, Te Heikiki and Reremai with their names. Kā mihi ki tōku whānau pūoro, and to my mātua pūoro, Ariana and Al. Thanks for showing me how pūoro can shape and change all things, and for gifting pūoro to the characters within me. Kā mihi ki tōku tuakana, Arihia Latham; I can't wait for this book to be next to Bird Speak back home. Thank you for always making me feel like I belong. To Gerry Te Kapa Coates for creating a path for our whānau back to our homelands of Te Wai Pounamu; I am so grateful to be in this whānau. Your work and strength has made all the difference to us and those who will come after. Thanks to Mum and Dad, for letting me run free in the wild, so I could write that freedom into Rere and Kiki.

Kā mihi aroha ki kā kaituhituhi Māori. I am so blessed for all the Māori writers I have been mentored by and grown up with. Thank you especially to essa and Michelle; I feel so lucky to be weaving words with you both, and to have you as test readers. Your aroha for our people is there in every word you write, thank you for always motivating me to do my best for us. Thank you to Lucy for being a test reader and listener for all my work, from when we were eleven years old, on to the end. Kā mihi ki te puna reo o Waihao mā, e Karuna. So privileged to have your eyes over this book before it went into the world and for your wisdom and dedication to our reo Kāi

Tahu. Kā mihi aroha ki a Isaac Te Awa; thank you for being an early reader of this book and affirming my view of te ao Māori and Te Wai Pounamu. Thank you for treating knowledge as a taoka and for gifting it to all our precious Kāi Tahu, Kāti Māmoe, and Waitaha whānau so that they know how worthy and special they are.

Kā tae o te raki, kā tae o te whenua, ka ora ai he mana whenua o Waihao! Thank you to Waihao marae and our Waihao whānau for embracing me with open arms and making it feel like I'd been home all along. Thank you for every kaputī, every mission to the box, every airport pick-up, every wānaka, every waiata, and every smoko. May this book whakamana our ancestors and show our Waitaha babies how precious they are within the aho of their ancestors.

And of course, kā mihi nunui ki te waiata tīmataka o te ao—thank you to the song that sung all that has made this book possible, into being.